A Kid's First Book of Gardening

Growing Plants Indoors and Out

Derek Fell

Running Press • Philadelphia, Pennsylvania

Canadian representatives: General Publishing Co., Ltd., 30 Lesmill Road, Don Mills, Ontario M3B 2T6.

International representatives: Worldwide Media Services, Inc., 115 East Twenty-third Street, New York, New York 10010.

Cover design by Toby Schmidt
Interior design by Stephanie Longo
Cover photographs by Derek Fell
Cover illustrations by Liz Vogdes, Eric Walker, and Patricia Perleburg
Interior illustrations by Jon Snyder

Photographs: Pages 58, 74, and 88, courtesy of W. Atlee Burpee & Co.; pages 1, 9 (right), 19, 21, 23, 26, 29, 32, 33, 37, 40, 48, 53, 57, 59, 62, 64, 65, 66, 69, 76, 89, 91, by Derek Fell; pages 9 (left), 17, and 82, courtesy Harris Seeds; page 38, Netherlands Board of Tourism.

9 8 7 6 5 4 3 2 1

Digit on the right indicates the number of this printing.

Library of Congress Cataloging-in-Publication Data
Fell, Derek.
  A kid's first book of gardening: growing plants indoors and out/ Derek Fell.
    p. cm.
  Includes bibliographical references.
  Summary: Presents information on soil, seeds, easy-to-grow flowers, flowers that keep blooming, bulbs, vegetables, fruits, trees, shrubs, houseplants, gardening in containers, and unusual plants.

ISBN 0-89471-750-2 : $9.95
  1. Gardening–Juvenile literature.
[1. Gardening.] I. Title.
SB457.F45   1989
635–dc20   89–43030
CIP   AC

ISBN 0-89471-750-2 (paperback)
    0-89471-751-0 (package)

This book may be ordered by mail from the publisher. Please add $2.50 for postage and handling for each copy. *But try your bookstore first!*
Running Press Book Publishers
125 South Twenty-second Street
Philadelphia, Pennsylvania 19103

To Vicky, Derek, Jr., and Tina

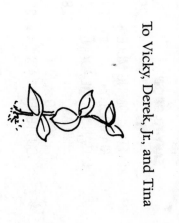

Contents

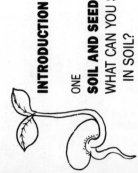

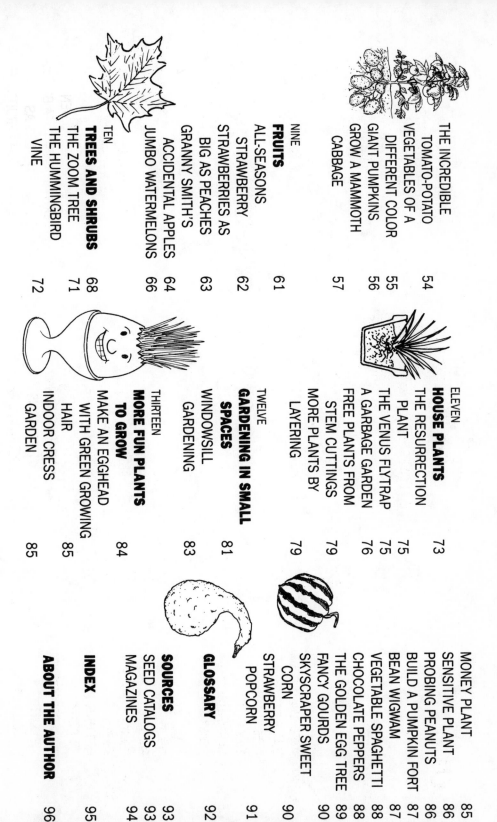

Introduction

To be happy all your life, be a gardener.

—Chinese Proverb

An ancient Greek legend tells of a strong man named Antaeus (an-TEE-us) who lived in a fertile valley and would not let anyone pass through. Hercules, the strongest man in the world, tried to pass, but every time Hercules threw Antaeus to the ground, Antaeus would jump up with increasing strength. Hercules learned that the secret of Antaeus's strength. Every time Antaeus touched the earth with his hands, he regained his strength and could beat all his enemies. When Hercules realized this he changed his tactics. He embraced Antaeus in a bear hug, lifted him clear of the soil, and won the fight.

When you start gardening, you may feel like Antaeus. Many people feel a sense of power, and also contentment, as soon as they begin working their fingers in the soil. You can scarcely realize the miracles which will take hold as a result of your efforts in this humble and noble product of nature called soil. By planting tiny seeds and caring for them, you can (with nature's help) produce all sorts of living

miracles—from tasty berries to towering trees that can live thousands of years.

Few experiences in life are more pleasurable than making the soil productive. As soon as your hands touch the soil and start to work with it, troubles seem to disappear.

Colorful flowers can lift our spirits, and pleasant herbal fragrances such as lavender and chamomile are soothing. Fresh fruits and vegetables are the best source of nourishment for our bodies. And the exercise we get from gardening—being out in the fresh air and working our muscles—keeps us fit.

a harvest of onions

tending the family garden

Gardening can be a family affair You can grow vegetables and herbs for family meals, and flowers to brighten your home and garden. Everybody in the family can help.

What other activity is as healthy, satisfying, and creative as cultivating a garden? From a small patch of earth you can grow tomatoes the size of grapefruits, strawberries as big as peaches, mammoth cabbages, and everblooming marigolds. You can plant a tree that grows eight feet a year and a houseplant whose leaves turn from dried-up brown to healthy green within minutes after adding water

It's all here in this book—the fun and fundamentals of gardening, plus a lot of exciting surprises.

—Derek Fell

CHAPTER ONE

Soil and Seeds

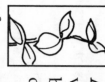

At first glance, what could be more boring than a clump of earth? Look again!

Soil is made up of many small particles. You can see them when you rub a clump of earth in the palm of your hand. You will also find living creatures such as earthworms that eat soil, pass it through their bodies, and expel it as waste. This waste is richer than the original soil and is a source of plant food. If you look at soil under a microscope, you will see that it contains other creatures called bacteria (bak-TEER-ee-uh). Like earthworms, bacteria produce plant food. In good soil—soil that is crumbly, fluffy, and moist—these creatures thrive, enriching the soil and helping plants produce bountiful harvests of vegetables and flowers.

Soil helps anchor plants. If soil is too light in texture (such as sand), plants are easily uprooted and the foods and moisture that plants need to grow drain away too quickly. In heavy soil (such as clay), plant roots have trouble pushing through and cannot make use of any plant food in the soil. The best soil is a mixture of coarse and fine soil particles called loam. Loam is rich in plant food because it contains humus (HEW-muss), a spongy material made up of decaying animal and plant matter. Humus makes air spaces in the soil that let bacteria and plant roots

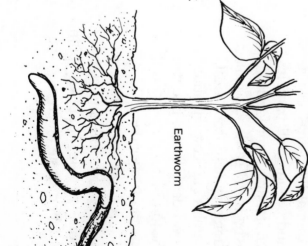

Earthworm

breathe. It also helps hold moisture in the soil.

In nature, plant and animal waste help make the soil rich. Leaves slowly decay and produce a dark, fluffy, soil-like material called leaf mold. Animal droppings also decay and become soil particles containing plant food. That's why many gardeners collect horse manure from local stables and cow manure from local dairy farms, pile it in a heap to let it decay, and then spread it over the soil.

A good way to improve your garden soil is to start a compost pile. Simply by piling kitchen waste (such as grape-fruit rinds and potato peelings) and garden debris (such as grass clippings, leaves, and weeds) into a corner of the garden, you can make your own fertilizer. The ingredients in your compost pile will turn into a dark, fluffy material that will feed hungry plants if you spread it over the soil.

This kind of soil improvement takes time. Many gardeners take shortcuts to improve their soil. Instead of using manure and compost to provide humus rich in plant food, they buy bales of peat from a garden center. Peat, or peat moss, is a light, fluffy material made of a decayed moss dug from deposits in the earth that are millions of years old. It helps hold moisture in the ground and leaves air spaces so that plant roots have room to grow.

Gardeners like to mix peat with a bag of fertilizer and add it to their garden soil. The combination of peat and fertilizer gives the soil a fluffy texture and adds plant food. Using peat and fertilizer is expensive, and it's not as good as natural soil improvement, but it's faster.

compost

WHAT CAN YOU SEE IN SOIL?

. . . .

Here's an experiment you can do to see what soil is made of.

Put a heaping handful of soil in a glass jar Fill the jar with water, close the lid tightly, and shake the soil and the water until the water is cloudy. Then let the jar stand so that the soil can settle.

After several hours you'll see that the largest soil particles have sunk to the bottom and the finest soil particles have settled on top Above the soil particles you may see a layer of fibrous pieces. This is

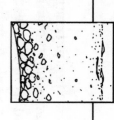

humus. On the surface of the water will be floating pieces of debris—perhaps some pieces of stem, leaves, seeds, or broken roots—that have not yet begun to decompose.

If the soil in your garden is made up mostly of very fine particles, then you have a clay soil. If the soil is made up mostly of coarse particles, you have a sandy soil. Good garden loam will have a balance of fine and coarse particles.

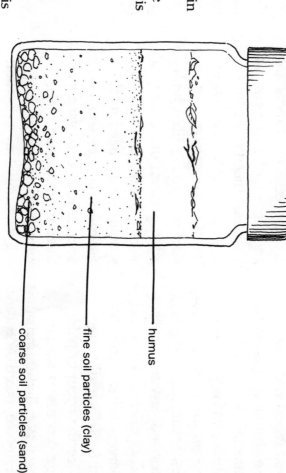

coarse soil particles (sand)

fine soil particles (clay)

humus

Seeds

The most common way that plants reproduce is by seeds. The seeds of some plants, such as petunias, are so tiny that when you hold them in the palm of your hand they look like specks of dust and will blow away if you even breathe on them. Other seeds, such as beans, are as big as marbles and easy to handle. The seeds of some trees are even larger—for example, coconuts are actually large seeds for the coconut palm.

The process of a seed sprouting is called germination (jer-muh-NAY-shun). You can't

tell just by looking at a seed whether it will sprout and produce a plant. Whether a seed germinates or not depends on its age and other conditions.

All seeds need moisture and air in order to germinate. They also need to be at the right temperature. Some seeds (such as cress seeds and peas) start to sprout within hours of adding water; others may take weeks. Some need light to sprout; others need total darkness. Lettuce seeds will germinate in cool weather, but tomato seeds need high temperatures.

The only way to be sure

that the seeds you buy have a good chance of sprouting is to buy them from a well-known company. Seed companies test a sample batch of seeds to see how many germinate, and this information is often printed on the seed packet. Read the seed packet before you plant—it should tell you what conditions the seeds need to germinate. (For a list of some good sources of seeds, see pages 93–94.)

GERMINATE

A

BEAN SEED
· · · · · · ·

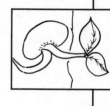

Here's an experiment that will show you how seeds germinate. Fill a glass jar with moist cotton or paper towels and place bean seeds around the sides. Any bean is good to use, but Fordhook lima beans are best because the seeds are extralarge. Then place the jar in a warm, dark part of the house. Keep the cotton or paper towels moist.

Within a few days you will see the seed coat swell and then split, as the plant sends out a root that grows down and a leafy shoot that

grows up. Soon the roots will fill the jar and the first leaves will appear.

Even if you plant seeds upside-down, the roots will always grow down toward the center of the earth, and the shoot will always grow up toward the sun.

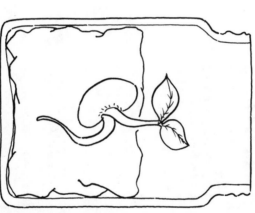

germinating bean seed

upside-down bean seed germinating

CHAPTER TWO

Planning
and
Planting

Anyone can have a garden. You don't need a lot of space to grow beautiful flowers and delicious vegetables. In fact, a small space that is well cared for can yield more than a large area that is neglected.

You can grow many flowers and vegetables in containers or window boxes. Some people buy wooden half-barrels at garden centers to use as planters. In just one half-barrel you can grow a dozen lettuce plants around the rim, and a tomato or pepper plant in the middle! Window boxes are good for

growing flowers, herbs, and salad greens. (For more about container gardening, see pages 82–83.)

If you have enough space to plant an outdoor garden, choose an area that gets plenty of sunlight—at least six hours a day, but the more the better. Also, make sure that the soil has good drainage. Soil with good drainage will absorb the water after a rainstorm. If the water forms puddles, then the soil has poor drainage. Ask your parents to help you find the best spot. (Be sure to get permission before you start digging!)

Tools

One of the good things about gardening is that it

Getting the Soil Ready

Once you've picked a site for your garden, dig the ground up with a spade or shovel, about a foot deep, and then rake it level. As you are digging and raking, remove any large stones, tough weed roots, or trash such as bottles and cans.

Try not to walk on freshly dug garden soil. If you have to walk on it in order to do your planting, put down a wooden board to spread your weight so you don't leave footprints.

doesn't require a lot of expensive equipment. You'll need just a few basic tools.

To grow plants in containers, all you'll need are a hand trowel (a small shovel) to dig the soil and a watering can to water the plants during dry spells.

For a regular garden, you'll need a spade (a large shovel), a rake to break up large clumps and level the soil, and a hand trowel to dig holes for planting and to dig out weeds. Wooden stakes and some string to stretch between them will help you plant seeds in straight rows. A wheelbarrow can also come in handy for

carrying plants, fertilizer, and bales of peat out to the garden. A pair of rubber boots will keep your sneakers or shoes from being ruined when you work in the garden on wet or dusty days.

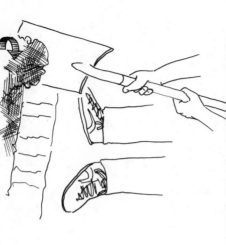

turning over the soil

Plan Before You Plant

Before you plant your garden, it's a good idea to plan it. Many gardeners like to draw a plan on paper On a sheet of graph paper, sketch the shape of your garden space Draw it so that each square on the graph paper equals one square foot of garden space. (Your parents can help you measure the garden.) Then you can mark where you want to plant different kinds of flowers or vegetables.

Be sure to leave enough space between rows of plants, and between the individual plants in each row. For most

flowers, leave one foot of space between each plant. Some large vegetable plants—such as tomatoes, summer squash, and pumpkins—need more space. (If you're planting seeds for large vegetables, check the seed packet to see how much space each type of plant needs.)

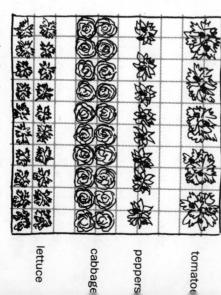

sample plan for a vegetable garden

lettuce

cabbage

peppers

tomatoe

By making a plan showing where each variety is to be planted, you'll know how many seed packets to use, or, if you'll be using ready-grown plants, how many plants to buy.

Planting the Seeds

Some seeds, such as corn and beans, can be planted directly into the garden. Others, such as petunias and begonias, are too small to be planted directly into the garden. They need to be started indoors in a seed tray and transferred to small pots when they are large enough to handle The plants can be transplanted outside when they have started to form flower buds, and when the weather is warm and sunny.

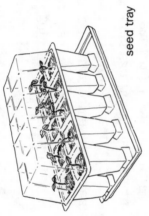

seed tray

For starting seeds indoors without the trouble of pots and soil, you can use a Jiffy-7 peat pellet. Made from peat compressed into a hard, round disc, it soaks up water like a sponge. It will expand to several times its original size and become soft and fluffy. Then you can plant seeds in the hollow area on top of the pellet. A little net holds the peat together, and plant roots can grow through the net. When it's time to put the plant outdoors, the pellet can be placed in the garden without disturbing the plant's roots.

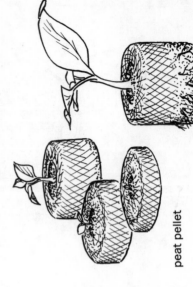

peat pellet

When planting seeds directly into the garden, the depth to plant them depends on the size of the seed. Fine seeds need very little soil coverage; the seed can be simply pressed into the upper soil surface. Large seeds should be planted at a depth about four times the width of the

seed. For example, a pea seed that measures a quarter-inch across should be planted one inch deep.

Seed packets explain how deep to plant seeds, and also how much space to leave between plants. For planting in rows, two measurements are given—the space between each plant in a row, and the space between rows of plants. For example, a packet may advise planting pea plants six inches apart, with three feet of space between the rows.

Usually, when planting seeds directly into the garden, you need to sow the seeds close to one another, because

not all the seeds will come up. You can thin out the plants after they come up if they are too crowded. If there are gaps in the rows, you can dig up seedlings (young plants) from a crowded section and plant them in the gaps. If you're using ready-grown plants, plant them in the garden at the exact spacing that you want, because transplants usually survive

The biggest mistake beginning gardeners make is trying to do too much. Remember that a small space, well cared for, can grow much more than a large area that is neglected.

CHAPTER THREE

Tending Your Garden

A little effort taken after planting will help your garden be a big success.

Mulch

After your seeds begin to sprout, you can prevent weeds from taking over your garden by putting down a layer of straw, grass clippings, wood chips, leaves, or other material. Gardeners call this mulch. Spread mulch around your plants after your seeds have come up and it will suffocate weeds. (Be careful not to cover your plants.) If a few weeds do

appear, just pull them out. Make sure you remove the roots or the weeds will grow back again.

Watering

Water your garden during dry spells. If a week goes by without rain, water the garden with a hose or lawn sprinkler. Your plants will then think they are having a good shower

Controlling Pests

Flower gardens are not as bothered by pests as vegetable gardens. If you have a vege-table garden, be on the look-

watering the garden

out for bugs and other pests that like to eat plants. Slugs and snails can kill young plants by eating them down to the bare stem, but they are not such a problem once your plants have started to fill out and flower If you see a lot of slugs and snails at planting time, sneak out early one morning and, wearing a pair of gloves, pick up any slugs and snails you can find and put them in a jar or bucket so you can get rid of them.

Don't use chemical sprays to control insects or disease. Always use an organic (or-GAN-ik), or natural, remedy. For example, if you see colonies of tiny sucking insects called aphids (AY-fidz) clustered around the stems, you can get rid of them with a blast of water from a hose fitted with a trigger-type nozzle. If caterpillars are a nuisance, a product called "BT" can be used. BT contains a type of bacteria that infects the bodies of caterpillars and kills them. These bacteria are harmless to people.

The best way to avoid diseases is to keep your plants healthy by regular watering during dry spells, by keeping the soil fertile, and by clearing the garden of old stems at the end of each growing season.

Easy-to-Grow Flowers

The easiest flowers to grow are annuals (AHN-yoo-ulz). Annuals are flowers that sprout from seed, grow, flower, and produce seeds for a new generation, all in one growing season.

Marigolds and zinnias (ZIN-ee-uhs) are especially easy to grow. The seeds can be planted directly into the garden during warm weather. They germinate in about five days, flower within six weeks, and continue flowering non-stop all summer until fall frost. A beautiful flower garden with marigolds and zinnias will provide armloads of

flowers to cut for bouquets and flower arrangements in your home. In fact, the more you pick the flowers of marigolds and zinnias, the more flowers the plants produce.

an annual flower garden

Some other easy-to-grow annual flowers are morning glories, asters, cornflowers,

Shirley poppies, calendulas (kuh-LEN-joo-luhz), and straw-flowers. All these flowers can be grown from seed. If you can spend the extra money for plants rather than seeds, go to your local garden center and buy ready-to-go transplants of snapdragons, scarlet sage, and petunias. For a shady area, plant begonias, impatiens (im-PAY-shunz), or coleus (KOH-lee-us).

asters

Everblooming Mule Marigolds

morning glories

A mule is the offspring of a male donkey and a female horse. When two types of animals or plants breed, the result is called a hybrid. The mule is a hybrid that has amazing strength and stamina. Mules helped pioneers settle America much more successfully than horses or donkeys could have.

Mule marigolds are a cross between the small French marigold and the tall American marigold. Like the mule, they are extra-strong.

Mule marigolds don't produce seeds. Instead, they direct all their energy into producing an astonishing number of flowers. As many as 50 to 100 flowers have been counted on one plant all at one time.

Mule marigolds bloom extra-fast—some varieties bloom just five weeks after the seeds are planted. The flowers may be yellow, orange, or red. Plant them in a sunny place for a magnificent garden display.

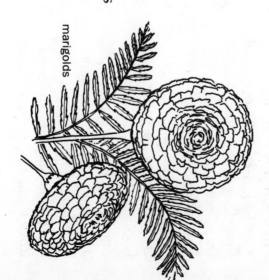

marigolds

Cut-and-Come-Again Zinnias

Many flowers don't like to be cut because it weakens the plant. But a family of zinnias called the "Cut-and-Come-Agains" just love it if you take a pair of scissors and snip off their flowers, because it makes them produce even more flowering stems.

Cut-and-Come-Again zinnias bloom in many beautiful colors: white, yellow, orange, pink, red, and purple. The lovely rounded flowers have long stems, so you can make beautiful big bouquets from them.

A bonus is the fact that zinnias attract butterflies, especially the magnificent swallowtail butterfly. You will see in the next section how to combine zinnias and marigolds to make a "butterfly garden."

Zinnias are very easy to grow from seed. Just scatter the seeds onto bare soil and rake them into the surface. Keep them moist, and within days the seeds will sprout. Zinnias usually flower within six weeks. They love a sunny spot and survive dry, hot summers better than most other flowers.

You can also buy zinnias

as plants from a garden center. If you do, look for young plants that have not yet started to flower. Zinnias don't like to have their roots disturbed, and a tall zinnia may wilt and die after transplanting.

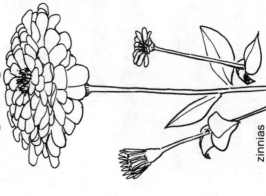

zinnias

An Easy-to-Plant Butterfly Garden

Butterflies love to visit certain plants, such as butterfly weed (a wildflower with bright orange flower clusters) and butterfly bush (a shrub with fragrant flowers that look like lilacs).

The easiest flowers to grow that attract butterflies are marigolds and zinnias, especially the bright orange and yellow marigolds and the bright red and pink zinnias. Plant a clump of these together in a sunny spot, and when they start to flower, watch for

swallowtail butterfly on impatiens

the many butterflies that like to visit them, including swallowtails, monarchs, and red admirals. Nature provides few more beautiful sights than butterflies fluttering over a bed of brightly colored flowers on a sunny day.

Here are some other plants that butterflies love to visit:

ANNUALS

asters
borage
cornflower
heliotrope
lantana
nasturtium

PERENNIALS

bergamot
loosestrife (lythrum)
milkweed
sedum
snakeroot

SHRUBS

blue mist shrub
buddleia
crape myrtle
Saint-John's-wort

CHAPTER FIVE

Flowers That Bloom Year after Year

Flowers that come back year after year from roots that rest in the soil through the winter are called perennials (puh-REN-ee-uhlz). Most perennials take two seasons to flower from seed. However, if you buy ready-grown plants from a local nursery or garden center, you usually save a year of growing time and can expect flowers the same season.

Some easy-to-grow perennials are peonies (PEE-uh-neez), chrysanthemums, Oriental poppies, phlox, coreopsis (KOR-ee-OP-sus), gaillardias (gay-LAR-dee-uhz),

Siberian irises (EYE-russ-ez), day lilies, sedums (SEE-dums), lilies, astilbe (uh-STILL-bee), and Shasta daisies. For these plants, it's best to use year-old container-grown plants from a garden center, so that your

day lily

plants will flower the same season you plant them.

Some perennials will flower the first year from seed—just like annuals—and then come up year after year to repeat their flowering display. Two such flowers are "Southern Belle," a hardy hybrid hibiscus (hih-BIS-kus), and "Pinwheel," a hybrid gloriosa (GLOR-ee-OH-suh) daisy.

Perennials usually spread out each year, making bigger and

iris

lily

"Southern Belle" hibiscus

Grow Flowers the Size of Dinner Plates

Hibiscus is a tropical plant that usually grows only in areas with warm winters, such as Florida and Southern California. However, a wild variety called the swamp mallow grows in swampy areas along the east coast of the United States. Plant breeders have used the swamp mallow to create a garden variety called "Southern Belle."

You can buy Southern Belle plants from garden centers in the spring, or you can grow your own from seed. If you grow them from seed,

plant the seeds indoors, six weeks before the last frost, so that you will have small plants to place outside after danger of frost. The seeds are about the

perennials with spreading root system

bigger clumps. This happens because the roots grow sideways and produce new plants in a circle that gets bigger every year In a few years you can take a spade and break up a big clump into lots of smaller ones. Then you can replant the clumps in other locations.

size of a small pea. They have a hard coat and need to be soaked in a glass of water overnight before planting to help germination.

Plant Southern Belle in a sunny location. The plants will start to flower in midsummer and continue to bloom until fall frosts. The individual flowers measure up to ten inches across.

Water the plants during dry spells. When frost arrives the plant will die down to the roots, but the roots will remain alive. When warm weather returns in spring, the plant will send up new leaves and flowering stems.

Gloriosa Daisies—
The Instant Perennials

The trouble with most perennials is that they take two years to bloom from seed. The first year they grow only leaves, storing up energy to flower the next year But not all perennials are so slow to flower A few will flower spectacularly the first season from seed.

A wildflower called black-eyed Susan grows along the waysides of every state from Alaska to Florida. It looks like a daisy, with orange petals and a black center The black-eyed Susan is a perennial, growing

leaves the first year and flowers the second. But plant breeders discovered how to turn it into an annual so that it flowers the first year At the same time, they succeeded in making the flowers up to three times larger

black-eyed susans (also known as gloriosa daisies

These new kinds of black-eyed Susans are so different from the wild kinds that they were given a new name, gloriosa daisies. The gloriosa daisy is so hardy and so easy to grow you can even sow seed on top of snow. As the snow melts, the seeds drop into cracks in the soil and sprout as soon as the soil warms up. By midsummer the plants will be flowering, and they will continue to flower until fall frosts. They then die down, rest over winter, and come back each year to flower again.

An All-Seasons
Perennial Border

Many annuals flower continuously all summer, but most perennials will flower for only two or three weeks. To keep a garden colorful with perennials, plant a lot of different kinds, mixing them so that when one plant goes out of bloom, one near it comes into bloom.

Below is a sample perennial border using plants with different blooming seasons so something is always coming into bloom.

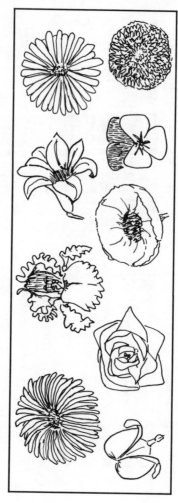

A perennial border garden
top; left to right: aster (fall bloom), iris (spring bloom), lily (summer bloom), daisy (summer bloom)
bottom; left to right: bleeding heart (spring bloom), rose (summer bloom), oriental poppy (spring bloom), violet (spring bloom), chrysanthemum (fall bloom)

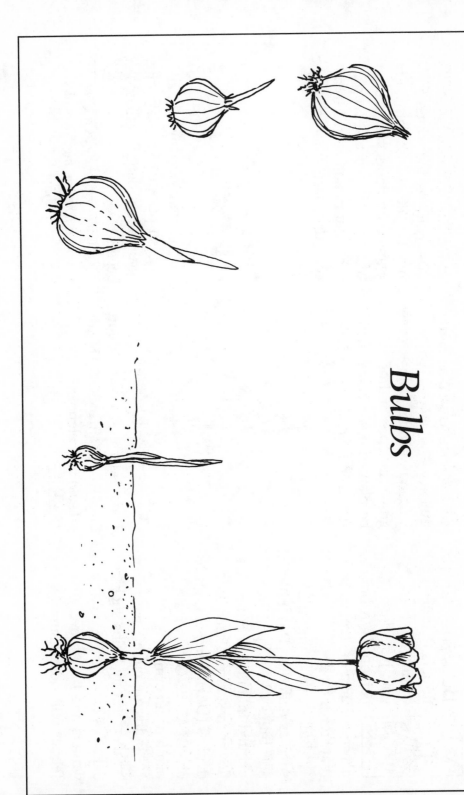

CHAPTER SIX

Bulbs

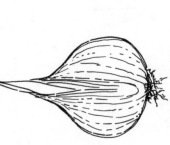

cross-section of a bulb

Bulbs produce flowers that keep coming up every year, just like perennials. A bulb is a swollen area of stem or root that stores food.

Bulbs that flower in spring, such as daffodils (DAF-uh-dilz) and tulips (TOO-lips), are planted in autumn. Bulbs that flower in summer, such as dahlias (DAHL-yuz) and gladioli (GLAD-ee-OH-lee), are planted in spring.

Bulbs are either "hardy" or "tender." Hardy bulbs such as daffodils can survive cold winters and bloom every year. Tender bulbs don't survive cold winters as well as hardy bulbs.

Some tender bulbs can be grown indoors, and others can be planted outside and then stored indoors for the winter

indoors as a houseplant to flower during the winter months. Elephant's ear can be planted outdoors after danger of frost and then taken up in the autumn and stored in a cool, dry place indoors for the winter

Two tender bulbs that are fun to grow are amaryllis (AM-uh-RIL-us) and elephant's ear. Amaryllis can be grown

Plant a Cloud of Daffodils

William Wordsworth, an English poet, wrote a famous poem about daffodils that begins

I wandered lonely as a cloud
That floats on high o'er vales
and hills,

When all at once I saw a crowd,
A host, of golden daffodils;
Beside the lake, beneath the trees,
Fluttering and dancing in the breeze.

Very few flowering plants are as dependable as the daffodil. Daffodils don't mind cold winters and faithfully bloom every spring, year after year. In fact, they are one of the first flowers to bloom in spring—even ahead of tulips.

You can grow daffodils just about anywhere, even in flowerpots and window boxes. They grow from bulbs that are pointed at one end.

To plant daffodil bulbs, simply dig holes about six inches deep and pop in the daffodil bulbs. You can plant them anytime between Labor Day and Christmas. Make sure the pointed ends of the bulbs face up and cover them with soil.

The following spring, they will flower with golden, trumpet-like blooms. Plant a lot—you may want to pick some for bouquets to display in vases around the house.

If you want to see daffodils multiply rapidly, plant them in a sunny spot with plenty of compost or peat in the soil, and feed them with a bulb fertilizer twice a year—in spring before the plants bloom, and again in fall. Follow the directions on the label for the amount to use

Tulips—A Favorite Flower of Sultans and Emperors

Tulips grow wild in desert-like areas of Turkey and

Siberia. When an Austrian traveler saw tulips growing in the gardens of a Turkish sultan in the 1500s, he was so impressed that he took tulip bulbs home to the Emperor of Austria for planting in the Imperial Gardens. When the emperor's gardener moved to Holland, he took tulip bulbs with him. Soon, nearly everyone in Holland with a garden wanted to grow them. They had never seen flowers in such beautiful colors, with petals that shimmered like satin. Because they bloom early in the spring, tulips made people happy after a long, bleak winter. The Dutch people

began to export tulips all over the world.

Planting tulips is easy. Like daffodils, tulips are hardy

Many tulips are imported from Holland (the Netherlands) where they grow in large fields.

bulbs. Choose a sunny day in fall to plant them—any time between Labor Day and Christmas. The bulbs are brown, rounded at the bottom and pointed on top. Just plant them six inches deep with the pointed side up. Space the bulbs four to six inches apart. For the best effect, plant them in clumps of 12 to 15 bulbs of all one color. They grow in sunlight or shade. Just be sure that the soil has good drainage.

To keep tulips coming back each year, leave the stems and leaves on the plant after the flowers have faded, but remove any seed heads that may develop. The leaves and stems help the bulb to replenish itself so it will flower again, but seed formation drains it of energy.

You'll find tulips in many shapes and sizes, and they have the widest color range of all flowering plants, even blooming in black and green! The most popular colors are red, yellow, pink, and orange.

The flower can be shaped like an egg, like a water lily, or like a peony. Some tulips have pointed petals and some (called parrot tulips) have petals shaped like a parrot's feather. Some tulips grow more than one flower on each stem.

Since the first tulips were introduced into Holland 400 years ago, more than 3,000 varieties have been produced by plant breeders, and 800 kinds are still available for gardeners to plant in their gardens.

Elephant's Ear

Elephant's ear is an exotic-looking plant that comes from Hawaii, but it will grow in any area with warm summers. Elephant's ear grows from a bulb that must be stored indoors during cold winter months.

Plant the bulb outdoors in the spring after all danger of

frost, and it will send up enormous heart-shaped leaves as big as elephant's ears. Elephant's ears grow as tall as six feet high.

Amaryllis

Amaryllis is a beautiful flowering bulb that can be grown indoors as a houseplant that will bloom in the winter In the spring, you can transplant it outside in your garden and it will bloom again. In frost-free areas of the United States, such as Florida and Southern California, amaryllis can be grown outdoors year-round.

Potted amaryllis bulbs can usually be found in your local supermarket anytime after Labor Day. All you need to do is place the pot in a sunny window and water daily. With-

in days the bulb will spring to life, producing a cluster of leaves, and then a tall, thick flower stem with a fat bud. The bud will open into a

amaryllis

elephant's ear

gorgeous cluster of four flowers, each one up to ten inches across. All this takes place within about six weeks. After the first flower cluster, another cluster may appear.

After the flowers have faded, keep the pot watered so the leaves stay green and healthy. In spring, after all danger of frost, transplant the bulb into the garden: take it out of its pot and cover it with soil in a place that is sunny or lightly shaded.

In the autumn, after the return of frosty nights, the leaves will wither and die. When this happens, dig up the bulb, clean it off, and store it indoors in a cool, dry place for about eight weeks. (A good place to keep it is in the vegetable bin in your refrigerator.) Then you can plant it in another pot, with potting soil, put it in a sunny window indoors and start watering. Soon, new flower stems should appear, and the plant will reward you with another set of spectacular flowers.

CHAPTER SEVEN

Herbs

Herbs are useful plants. Some have a pleasant fragrance (such as mint) or a pleasant flavor (such as anise). Some herbs can be used for healing—for instance, aloe (AH-low) helps to heal burns. Other herbs repel insects (wormwood) or produce beautiful dyes (blue indigo).

You might not know that herbs are useful by looking at the plants—in fact, you could easily mistake some of them for weeds—but people have discovered many uses for them over the years.

Some easy-to-grow herbs, such as scented-leaf geraniums,

make attractive houseplants. Others, like parsley, chives, and basil, grow well in a pot on a sunny windowsill and can be used to add flavor to foods.

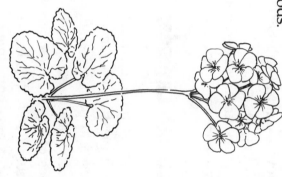

scented-leaf geranium

Deodorizer Plants

Some attractive herbs with decorative leaves release pleasant fragrances. These "deodorizer plants" are members of the geranium family (which includes the flowering geranium used in summer flower gardens), and are sometimes called "scented-leaf geraniums."

The leaves of deodorizer plants are usually velvety in texture, and are sometimes shaped like ivy leaves. They have a rich assortment of fragrances; they may smell like lemons, pineapples, coconuts, roses, or apples.

wonderful. Just one flower, or a small piece of stem with a few leaves, is enough to produce the fragrance.

You can start your own lavender plants from seed, or

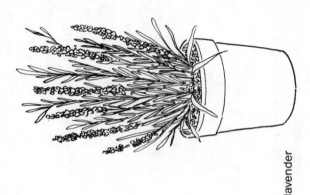

lavender

Scented-leaf geraniums are attractive houseplants, and they are very easy to grow. All you need is a pot and a sunny windowsill. They are not fussy about soil and can survive long periods without water. They grow best if you plant them in a regular houseplant potting soil (such as Jiffy-Mix) and water them whenever the soil feels dry.

If you have an unpleasant odor on your fingers (perhaps from handling fish or onions), just pick a leaf and rub it between your fingers and it will replace the bad smell with its own sweet fragrance.

The leaves also add flavors

to food. The next time your mother bakes muffins or popovers, ask her to place one leaf of a scented-leaf geranium at the bottom of each cup. When the muffin or popover is removed, the leaf will be cooked into the bottom, creating a beautiful design and adding a pleasant flavor.

Old English Lavender

Lavender produces one of the most pleasant fragrances, often used in perfumes and soaps. The plant also grows bunches of lovely blue flowers all summer long. The leaves and the flowers both smell

you can grow small, ready-grown transplants from a garden center Lavender plants like lots of sun, so plant them in a pot on a sunny window-sill, or outdoors in a sunny part of the garden.

Lavender plants are not fussy about soil, as long as it drains well, and they don't need watering until the soil feels dry. What's more, you need to plant them only once—they will survive winter and come back year after year

The leaves and flowers of lavender also make a re-freshing tea. Simply place an inch of stem with leaves—or a single flower—in a teacup and pour on hot water Let it stand for a minute, add a little sugar to sweeten it, and the tea is ready to drink. You also might like to add some flowers or sprigs of lavender to bath water to make it smell pleasant.

A Windowsill Herb Garden

Some herbs are perfect for growing in window boxes, or in pots on a sunny windowsill. Parsley, chives, and a type of basil called Green Ruffles Italian basil all grow well indoors.

Extra Curly parsley produces lots of tasty, dark-green leaves. Pick the outer leaves and the crown will grow more fresh green sprigs for a continuous harvest. For a tasty snack, chop up some parsley leaves, add them to cream cheese or butter, and spread it on toast or crackers. Parsley also adds flavor to fish dishes, eggs, sauces, potatoes, and pasta.

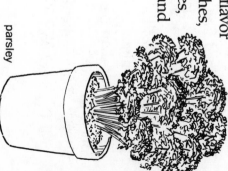

parsley

chives

basil

Zesty chives are onion-like plants that produce narrow, pointed leaves and clusters of bright pink flowers. They don't need any care other than regular watering when the soil gets dry. If the plants start to overcrowd the pot, you can break them into clumps and replant some of the clumps in other pots. Their decorative leaves, chopped fine, add flavor to eggs, potatoes, salads, and soups.

Green Ruffles Italian basil looks more like a gorgeous coleus plant than basil, but touch its exotic leaves and it releases that unmistakable basil fragrance to reveal its true identity. The plants are easy to grow. Keep picking the outer leaves, and more inner leaves will form to replace them. Basil is delicious on pizza—just chop up the leaves and sprinkle them over a slice.

These herbs are easy to grow from seed. You can buy seeds through mail-order seed catalogs. Some seed companies specialize in herbs, and will even send you plants by mail. You can find their addresses in the classified section of any good gardening magazine

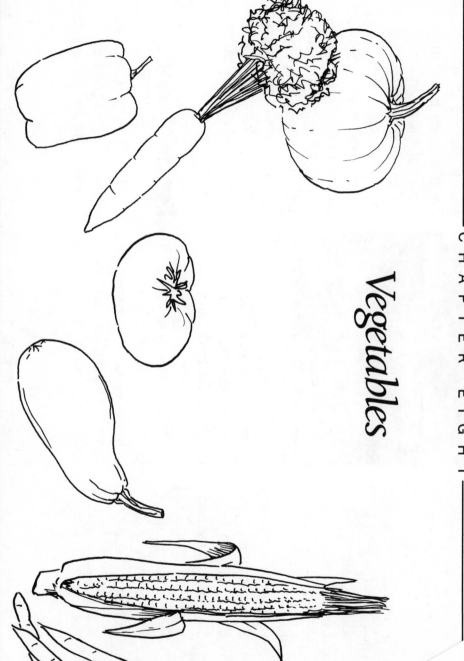

Vegetables

find out about community garden projects in your neighborhood by calling a local botanical garden for information, or by calling your local county agent, usually listed in the Human Services section of the Yellow Pages. Part of the job of a county agent is to help people with questions about farming and gardening. Your state horticultural society also might be able to help.

Beware of Frost

The most important things to know before planting a vegetable garden are the dates

a harvest of sweet corn

grown in containers on patios or on windowsills. (For more on container gardening, see pages 82–83.)

Many cities give young people an opportunity to cultivate gardens by providing space on vacant lots and in botanical gardens. You can

You'll find vegetables in all shapes and sizes. There are leafy vegetables (such as lettuce, cabbage, and spinach); root vegetables (such as radishes, carrots, and beets); and fruiting vegetables (such as tomatoes, peppers, and zucchini).

Some vegetables are more fun to grow than others, especially those that can be encouraged to grow huge and maybe even win prizes at local garden shows. In this chapter, you'll see how to grow giant pumpkins, tomatoes, and cabbages.

Many vegetables can be

of the last frost in spring and the first frost in fall. The period in between is known as your "frost-free" growing season.

It's very important to know these dates because tender vegetables (such as tomatoes) must not be planted outside until after all danger of frost. When frost threatens to return in fall, you must harvest all your tender vegetables or the frost will spoil them.

To find out your first and last frost dates, ask a teacher, a friend of the family who is a gardener, or a salesperson in a local garden center.

An Easy-Care Vegetable Garden

With a little care, it's easy to have a productive vegetable garden. Be sure to locate it in a sunny place where the soil has good drainage.

The most important requirements for a bountiful vegetable garden are fertile soil, enough water during dry spells, mulching to prevent weeds, and some common-sense pest control (such as washing off colonies of insects from plant stems when you see them appear).

Some vegetables are

especially easy to grow because the seeds can be planted right into the garden and will sprout soon after being covered with soil. Peas, beans, and corn all can be sown directly into the garden. With a little care, in just 60 to 90 days from planting you will have ripe vegetables to pick and eat.

Other vegetables, such as tomatoes, peppers, and cabbage, grow slowly from seed and should be set into the garden as young plants.

Leafy vegetables (such as lettuce) need to be planted early in spring so they mature during cool weather; others (such as tomatoes) need to be planted after frost because they are tender and need warm days to mature. Check the seed packets before planting to see when the best time to plant is.

Most seed companies supply enough seed in their packets to sow a 15-foot row, so the easiest way to plan your garden is in rows 15 feet long.

Instead of growing all your vegetables in single rows, you can save space by planting raised double rows of vegetables that do not get big, such as lettuces and beans. Larger vegetables such as peppers and tomatoes can still be planted in single file along the raised row.

To make a raised double row, pile the soil six inches high and two feet-wide with your spade. You can use a ruler to make sure you have two-foot-wide raised rows, with one-foot walkways between the rows. Since you never grow anything in a walkway, you can take soil from the walkway and use it to make the raised double rows. Then plant two rows of vegetables along the raised area.

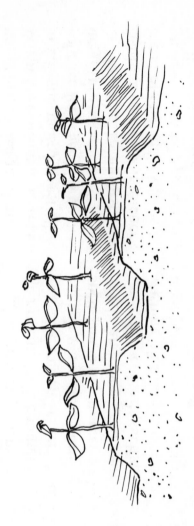

Raised double rows allow you to plant more vegetables in the same amount of space.

To make straight rows, use string stretched tight between stakes. You will need a set of four wooden stakes to mark each corner of the raised bed. They should be at least 12 inches long. Push them halfway into the soil. Space them in pairs two feet apart at each end of the raised row, and stretch string in two parallel lines to make the edges of the row.

If you lay out your vegetable garden like this, it will be easier to care for. Your vegetables will like the extra soil depth, and you will never have any problem knowing exactly where to water and add fertilizer.

The planting plan shown here is just a suggestion. If you don't like lettuce and would prefer carrots, make the switch. Or, if you would rather grow melons than tomatoes, go ahead.

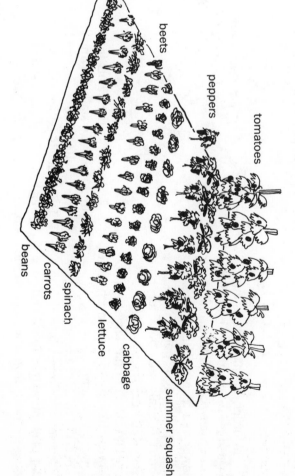

sample vegetable garden

beets

peppers

tomatoes

beans

carrots

spinach

lettuce

cabbage

summer squash

PLAY THE PART OF A BEE · · · · · ·

In order for many fruits and vegetables to grow, bees must help to transfer pollen from a male flower to a female. This process, called pollination (pol-ih-NAY-shun), is easily seen on a zucchini (zew-KEE-nee) squash vine.

The zucchini has large yellow flowers. It's easy to distinguish male flowers from female flowers, especially in the early morning, when squash flowers bloom. You can play the part of a bee and transfer pollen from the male to the female to grow a zucchini squash. Here's what to do:

1. When the vine begins to flower, look at the flowers. If the flower has a baby zucchini squash where the stalk is attached to the flower, it's a female. If it has no baby squash, just a stalk, it's a male

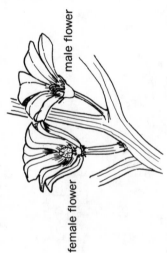

female flower

male flower

2. Peel away the petals from around the male stalk, leaving a powdery yellow "nose" exposed. This powder is pollen. The female flower has no pollen, just a shiny nose.

3. Rub the powdery nose of the male onto the shiny nose of the female. The pollen grains will stick to the female.

4. Within days the female flower should drop away. The zucchini will enlarge so you can pick it and eat it.

By transferring pollen from the male flower to the female, you gave birth to a zucchini.

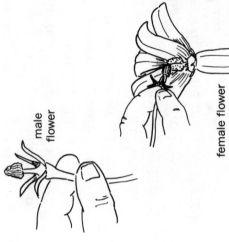

male flower

female flower

Grow Tomatoes as Big as Grapefruits

Tomatoes can grow so big that one slice will cover a whole slice of bread. Large tomatoes are often the tastiest ones, too.

Supersteak tomatoes

Of course, not all tomatoes can grow to giant size. It's important to select the right variety. Get one of the giant-size types, such as "Supersteak." Supersteak is a hybrid that grows smooth, round, and meaty tomatoes up to two pounds or more in weight. You may be able to find ready-grown Supersteak transplants at a local garden center. Or, you can buy seeds from a mail-order catalog and start your own.

Plant Supersteak tomato plants outdoors in a sunny place after all danger of frost, and keep them watered during dry spells. Feed the plants every two weeks with a high-phosphorus fertilizer, such as bone meal, and watch the plants grow loads of fruit, sometimes as large as grapefruits.

Supersteak plants tend to grow tall, so you may want to stake them—place a thin pole in the ground next to the plant to help support it. Another way to support the plant is by using builder's wire. Ask your parents to help you place a circle of wire around the plant. This way, the tomato plant's branches will push through the spaces in the wire, and the wire will hold the plant up when it starts to get heavy with plump tomatoes. Pick the tomatoes as they ripen and Supersteak will continue bearing all summer until fall frost. If you let all the fruit ripen at one time, you may need a wheelbarrow to carry them all to the kitchen!

Other types of giant tomatoes include:

Beefsteak Beefmaster hybrid
Ponderosa Bragger hybrid
Delicious Mr Lincoln

The Incredible Tomato-Potato

You can grow plants that have luscious red tomatoes ripening above ground and plump, red-skinned potatoes below ground.

Tomatoes and potatoes are very closely related. In fact, they look so similar in the garden you can hardly tell the difference between a tomato plant and a potato plant when they are young. The trick to growing tomato-potatoes is to graft a tomato plant onto a potato, and here's how to do it:

Take any red-skinned potato, such as the variety Red Pontiac, and hollow out a hole all the way through the middle with an apple corer or knife. The hole must be large enough to make room for the roots of a small tomato plant. Push the roots of the tomato plant into the hole, keeping as much soil around the roots as possible. Then plant the two together into fertile soil in a sunny location, making sure the potato is covered with soil and the tomato plant is above ground. Water immediately, and keep moist until the tomato plant grows strong and leafy.

Usually, the potato part of the graft is stronger, and at first it may send out leafy shoots around the edges that threaten to suffocate the tomato plant. If that happens, thin out the potato shoots by cutting off the biggest stems so the tomato plant can get enough air and light.

Eventually, the tomato plant will start to flower and fruit. After the tomatoes have ripened and you have harvested them, then you can dig up the entire plant and harvest up the potatoes.

Invite your friends and neighbors to see your tomato-potato. They won't believe their eyes when you harvest the last of your tomatoes and then dig up the soil to reveal plump red potatoes growing from the roots.

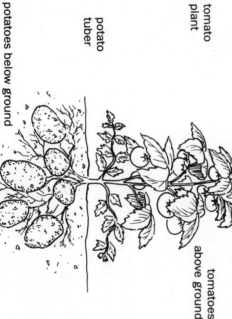

tomato plant

potato tuber

potatoes below ground

tomatoes above ground

Vegetables of a Different Color

A boy who shared a Chicago community garden with other children complained that when his vegetables were nearly ripe, someone would pick them before he had a chance to enjoy the harvest himself.

His teacher had an idea—instead of growing vegetables with colors everyone recognizes, why not grow some vegetables with unusual colors? Then, other children would either be afraid to pick them for fear of the vegetables being poisonous, or else they would be unable to tell when the vegetables were really ripe.

So, with the help of his teacher, here's what the boy decided to grow:

GOLDEN BEETS. Instead of red beets, he grew golden beets. They are bright orange in color. The beets don't bleed like red beets when they are cooked and sliced. They taste like red beets, and the leaves are delicious when cooked like spinach.

PURPLE-PODDED BEANS. The variety "Royal Burgundy" has dark purple pods that change color to bright green when you cook them. They're as tasty as regular snap beans.

PURPLE-HEADED CAULIFLOWER. It tastes like white cauliflower, but it's more nutritious.

WHITE CUCUMBERS. The color is as white as snow. The skin is so tender you don't need to peel it like a green cucumber, and inside it tastes cool and delicious.

RED-LEAF LETTUCE. Red cabbage has been around for a long time, but red lettuce is something new. Actually, when you strip off the leaves of red lettuce to make a salad, you'll find the heart is green like regular lettuce—just the tops of the leaves are bright red. They're as crisp and delicious as green lettuce.

BLACK BELL PEPPERS. Most bell peppers ripen green, red, or yellow. But now you can also grow black bell peppers. If you close your eyes, you can't tell the difference in flavor between a black bell pepper and a regular bell pepper.

BLUE POTATOES. You'll always find white potatoes and red-skinned potatoes in the supermarket produce section, but now you can grow blue potatoes. What's more, they're blue all the way through! They're especially delicious baked in their jackets.

BLACK RADISHES. There are two kinds of black radishes – round ones and long, pointed ones. Round black radishes are especially easy to grow. Inside, they're white and crisp, and their flavor is hotter than regular red or white radishes.

WHITE TOMATOES. Yes, there's a variety called "White Beauty" that's white all the way through. It has a milder flavor than a red tomato.

YELLOW WATERMELONS. The variety "Yellow Baby" can be planted earlier than other kinds, and it has half as many seeds as a regular watermelon. The inside is as yellow as a pineapple and extra sweet and

white tomatoes

delicious. In China, yellow watermelons are more common, and people will pay a higher price for a yellow watermelon because they like its sweeter flavor

Giant Pumpkins

Did you know that the world record for a giant pumpkin is now more than 600 pounds? For a pumpkin to grow that big, it has to increase in size at the rate of more than six pounds a day.

There's fierce competition among pumpkin growers. A record-breaking pumpkin can win prizes up to $10,000! Here's how the champions grow their pumpkins so big:

1. First, choose a variety that grows large, such as "Atlantic Giant."

2. Sow the seeds into the garden after all danger of frost

and water the plants *every day*. Pumpkins increase their weight by absorbing moisture from the soil through their roots. Only by watering the soil daily will you supply enough moisture to grow a large pumpkin.

3. Pumpkins like a soil with plenty of humus, especially well-decomposed animal manure. Also, pumpkin vines like a lot of nitrogen, so put a high-nitrogen fertilizer into the soil at planting time. This makes the vines grow long and healthy. The bigger the vine, the bigger the pumpkin it can grow.

4. Allow lots of small pumpkins to grow on the vines. When several of them are the size of tennis balls, examine them for a thick stem. Only pumpkins with thick stems attached to the vine will be able to absorb enough moisture to grow huge. When you've decided which pumpkin looks the best, pick off all the other fruit so that the vine puts all its energy into growing one extra-big pumpkin.

To prevent someone from stealing your giant pumpkin, you can put your name on it. When the pumpkin is big, just take a sharp knife and scratch the orange skin with your name. The scratch will form a blister that will raise the letters and make your name easy to read.

prize-winning pumpkins

You can find out about pumpkin-growing contests in your area by calling your local county agent's office. Usually, the county agent will be involved as an organizer or as a judge in the pumpkin contest.

If you grow a really big pumpkin, your local newspaper might even send over a photographer to take your picture.

giant cabbage

Grow a Mammoth Cabbage

The world's largest cabbage, grown in Scotland, was 113 pounds! Alaska is also famous for its giant cabbages. Cabbages like lots of sunlight and they like the long, cool days that occur close to the North Pole. During summer in Alaska and Scotland, it never gets completely dark at night, so the plants get plenty of sunlight.

Although you may not be able to grow the monster cabbages that gardeners in Alaska and Scotland grow, you can still grow a whopper that

will amaze your friends and might even win a prize at a local garden show.

The most important part of growing a giant cabbage is to choose the right variety—either "O.S. Cross" hybrid or "Heavyweighter." The seeds should be started indoors about eight or nine weeks before your last expected frost date. Cabbage plants can survive a little frost, so you can transplant the young plants into your garden two or three weeks before your last expected frost date

Plant your cabbages in soil with lots of compost mixed in. Cabbages like a fertilizer high in nitrogen, such as bone meal.

They also like plenty of moisture, so make sure to keep the soil watered.

Watch for the eggs of white butterflies (called "cabbage butterflies") among the leaves, because these will hatch into little green worms that can eat your cabbages down to skeletons. Inspect your plants every day and wash away the egg clusters before they have a chance to hatch into little green caterpillars with big appetites.

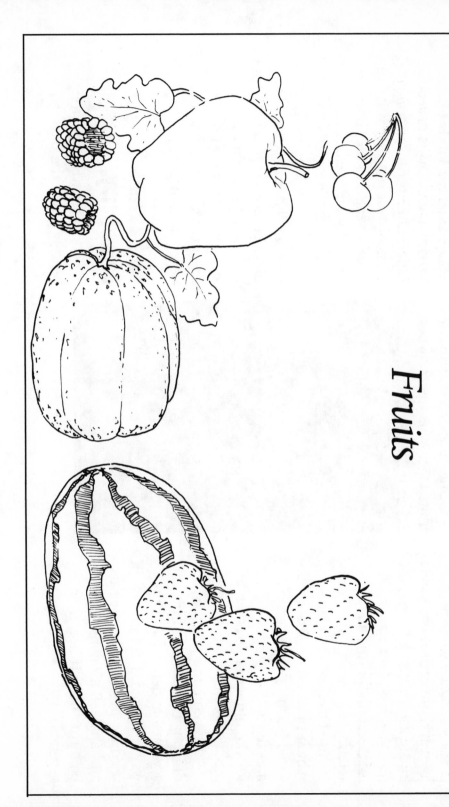

CHAPTER NINE

Fruits

<D> Do you know the difference between a fruit and a vegetable? To plant scientists, there isn't any difference. The word "fruit" can be used to describe plants which produce dessert-quality fruits (such as strawberries) and those that produce foods for the dinner table (such as tomatoes).

However, the popular difference between a fruit and a vegetable depends on the way it is used. If a fruit can be used for dessert (like melons and apples), it's considered to be a true fruit; if not, it's a vegetable.

One of the most popular fruits to grow is the strawberry.

There are three kinds of strawberries. One kind is called the June-bearer because in most parts of North America it fruits once a year, in June. The second kind is called the everbearer. The everbearer doesn't really keep bearing continually, but it does produce two crops a year—one in June and another in autumn. The third kind is the day-neutral strawberry, and it never stops bearing.

All-Seasons Strawberry

Most strawberries stop bearing when the days get

longer in summer, but the day-neutral strawberry is not affected by day-length. It produces a large crop of berries in June, several flushes of fruit in summer, and another heavy crop in autumn. As long as it's kept watered and fertilized it keeps on bearing. Another name for the day-neutral strawberry is the all-seasons strawberry.

A variety called "Tri-Star" is the best of the day-neutral strawberries. It was developed by Dr. Gene Galleta, a U.S. government strawberry breeder.

Usually, you need to order Tri-Star plants from a mail-order catalog. As soon as they

arrive, plant them with their roots spread apart and the

strawberry planter

crown with its neck just above the soil surface.

Within just 60 days you can expect to pick ripe fruit, and continue picking all season until fall frosts. Then the strawberries take a well-deserved rest. In the spring, they start growing again to

bear another continuous crop of luscious, sweet berries.

Strawberries as Big as Peaches

If you really want to amaze your friends, try growing a

crown
roots

large-fruited variety of strawberry such as "Earliglow," developed by the U.S. Department of Agriculture.

Strawberries prefer to be planted in full sun into fertile soil that has good drainage. The plants should be spaced 12 inches apart, with two to three feet between each row of plants. To prevent weeds, put a layer of leaves or straw around the plants. (They're called "strawberries" because people use straw to keep down weeds.)

It takes patience to grow really big strawberries. Pick all the flowers off during the first year, so that all the plant's energy goes into growing a strong root system. The next year it will astonish you by growing strawberries the size of small peaches.

Granny Smith's Accidental Apples

The world's most popular apple is the "Granny Smith." It's not red like a "McIntosh"

or yellow like a "Golden Delicious," but as green as grass. People like to eat these apples fresh, or to use them for cooking. Their flavor is sweet and juicy, with just the right amount of tartness. The Granny Smith keeps its fresh flavor for months, while other apples turn soft and taste like sawdust.

The Granny Smith was an incredible accident of nature. In 1869, Mrs. Thomas ("Granny") Smith of Australia discarded some rotten apples she had brought from the island of Tasmania onto her compost pile. A tree grew from the seed of the discarded fruit,

and it bore a shiny, green, scrumptious apple that her friends and neighbors called "Granny Smith's." Soon, a local apple grower heard about Granny Smith's special apple and took cuttings from it to grow trees in his own orchard. He didn't think it had much chance of selling because green apples were considered to be ugly ducklings.

But the fame of Granny Smith's apples started to spread. Soon, apple growers all over Australia were exporting the fruit to New Zealand and then to England, the home of some of the world's finest apples. "Granny Smith's"

completely won over the English and became their favorite apple. Now it is becoming number one in the United States as well.

The original Granny Smith apple takes a long time to ripen. In northern states it is best left on the tree until fall frosts, long after other apples have finished bearing. However, some apple nurseries have developed new strains of the Granny Smith with fruit that ripens much earlier, and trees that stay short so you don't need a stepladder to reach the fruit. These short trees are called "dwarfs," and they can be grown in tubs on a deck or patio.

dwarf Granny Smith apple tree

When Mrs. Smith threw a bag of rotten apples onto her compost heap, she had no idea that a tree would grow to make her name famous. Accidents in nature like this—where a plant grows something different—are called "mutations." Many mutations are of no value, but once in a while something special comes up and a new fruit, flower, or vegetable is born.

Jumbo Watermelons

Watermelons are a popular summer fruit that grows fast during hot, sunny weather.

The secret to growing a really big watermelon is choosing the right variety, such as "Royal Jubilee" or "Royal Windsor." With these varieties you may be able to grow a watermelon as heavy as 100 pounds! From seed to harvest they need about 80 days of warm weather.

Plant the seed one inch deep after all danger of frost. The plants will grow much faster and produce bigger fruit if a layer of black or clear plastic is spread over the soil to keep it extra warm.

The soil should be fertile, preferably with plenty of humus mixed in (especially humus in the form of well-decomposed animal manure). To grow really big, watermelons need lots of moisture, so keep the soil watered.

When the vines start to flower, examine them carefully to see when the first fruit starts to form. Then remove all other fruit so the plant's energy goes into growing one extra-large fruit. Giant water-melons take up a lot of room, so give them plenty of space. Two vines are generally enough, spaced about six feet apart.

It's sometimes tricky telling when a watermelon is ripe. One way is to examine the tendril (the curly stem) closest to the fruit. When the tendril turns brown, the watermelon is usually ripe. Another way to test ripeness is to tap the fruit with your knuckle and listen to the sound: If it's a dull sound the watermelon is under-ripe; if it's a hollow sound, the watermelon is ripe; and if it's a soft sound, the watermelon is over-ripe.

CHAPTER TEN

Trees and Shrubs

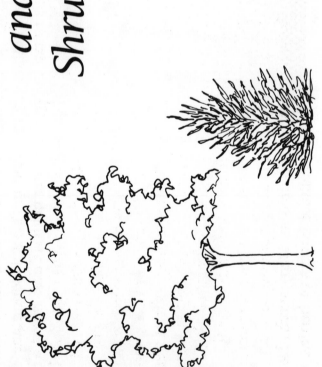

Trees and shrubs are both members of a plant family called "woody plants" that grow a strong, long-lasting cell structure called wood.

You can tell trees and shrubs apart by their appearance and height. A tree is usually defined as any woody plant capable of growing more than 15 feet high and having one main trunk. A shrub generally stays below 15 feet, and instead of one main trunk, a shrub has many stems, or multiple trunks.

Trees and shrubs can live for a very long time. There are

giant redwood forest

trees in California–such as the bristlecone pines of the White Mountains and the giant sequoias (suh-KWOY-uhz) of the Sierra Nevada mountains– that are thought to be more than 3,000 years old. In the Sonora Desert of California, there is a creosote bush (a shrub) that is estimated to be more than 10,000 years old, and in Pennsylvania, plant scientists have discovered a huckleberry bush that may be more than 13,000 years old.

Trees are good for providing shade, growing fruits such as apples or pears, and for decoration. A pair of trees spaced ten feet apart is perfect for hanging a hammock. Some trees bloom with beautiful blossoms in the springtime. Shrubs are mostly used for decoration. Many shrubs have beautiful flowers or berries.

They also make good hedges and windbreaks, keeping the wind from blowing topsoil away.

Trees and shrubs can be deciduous (deh-SIJ-ew-us) or evergreen. Deciduous trees and shrubs drop their leaves in the winter Many deciduous trees turn beautiful colors in the autumn as cold weather causes changes in their leaves. Maples, for instance, turn from bright green to deep red before they lose their leaves and take a rest for the winter

Evergreens are trees that can survive the winter without losing their leaves. Some are called needle evergreens because their leaves are very narrow. Pines and spruce are both needle evergreens. They stay green all year round and have narrow, pointed leaves like needles. Other evergreen trees and shrubs are called broadleaf evergreens. Rhododendrons and hollies are good examples of this group. Their leaves are wide and large compared to the needle evergreens. Both needle evergreens and broadleaf evergreens are especially good for creating windbreaks and hedges.

maple tree (deciduous)

maple leaf

pine tree (evergreen)

The Zoom Tree

Trees are generally considered to be fast growing if they grow two or three feet a year, but new hybrids have been created that grow even faster.

Plant scientists started looking for faster-growing trees to cover bare slopes that had been exposed by strip mining, where entire mountainsides are stripped bare of plants. They turned to the poplar tree, which can grow in poor soil. By crossing American poplars with poplars native to Europe (there are more than 30 different kinds of poplars in the world), scientists developed hybrid poplars that can grow up to eight feet a year.

Some of these new poplars were found to be good for beautifying yards. One such tree is the Androscoggin (an-droh-SKOG-in), which grows into a beautiful shade tree up to 50 feet high. The incredibly fast growth of this shade tree can be measured with a ruler from week to week. It grows more in a month than most other trees grow in an entire year

Super fast-growing hybrid poplars like the Androscoggin can be purchased through the mail from specialist nurseries. What you will receive is a one-year-old plant, called a sapling. Just plant it in ordinary garden soil, water it regularly, and watch it take off! When it has formed a thick trunk, you can even put a plaque on the tree with your name and the date when the tree was planted.

You can also plant a hybrid willow tree that grows at the astonishing rate of 12 feet a year Produced in Australia by crossing different kinds of willow trees, the hybrid Australian willow is new to the United States.

The Hummingbird Vine

Hummingbirds love nectar—a sweet liquid found at the centers of flowers. They are also attracted to the color red. Of all of the red flowers in the world, none attracts hummingbirds as much as the hummingbird vine, also called the trumpet vine or trumpet creeper. The hummingbird vine produces clusters of orange-red, trumpet-shaped flowers in summer. Hummingbirds like to poke their long, curving beaks into the centers of the flowers and drink the sweet nectar.

The hummingbird vine is also one of the fastest-growing shrubs in the world, often growing ten feet or more in a single season.

The plant requires no special care. It grows in good or poor soil, in sun or light shade, coast to coast, from Florida to Maine. The hummingbird vine will grow sideways along a fence, or up a trellis. It grows as tall as a person in a matter of weeks and can grow as tall as a house by the end of the first season.

Some people like to plant the hummingbird vine next to the house, so that its leaves grow up the walls and around

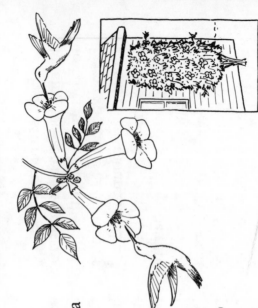

the windows. If you do this, you might wake up one morning and see families of hummingbirds enjoying a breakfast of nectar from the beautiful red flowers that bloom all summer

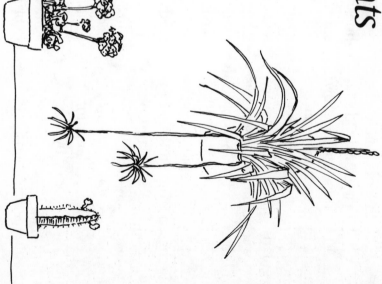

CHAPTER ELEVEN

Houseplants

You can grow a lot of interesting plants indoors. Many plants that grow wild out-doors can be grown inside in pots. If they get enough light, are watered regularly, and fertilized every two weeks, most houseplants will thrive and help to beautify the home.

Many houseplants can be purchased from stores. Most supermarkets have a display of plants, usually near the produce section. You can grow your own houseplants for much less money by starting from seeds. Coleus, cactus, geraniums, impatiens, and petunias are all easy to grow from seed.

The easiest way to grow houseplants from seed is to sprinkle the seeds onto an absorbent paper towel that has been moistened. Keep them in a warm, dark place and check them every day to see if the seeds have sprouted. Once the seeds sprout, plant them in individual pots. Some large seeds such as asparagus fern and bird of paradise can be sown directly into pots because their seeds are easy to handle.

If you would rather grow something to eat, try "Pixie" hybrid tomato as a houseplant.

Pixie grows in a pot and doesn't need as much light as other tomatoes to ripen its tasty fruit, which are about the size of golf balls. If you have a sunny, south-facing window, you usually can grow Pixie, even during winter months.

pixie hybrid tomato

The Resurrection Plant

The resurrection (rez-uh-REK-shun) plant grows wild throughout the southern United States and in Mexico. It grows on stones and along the branches of trees. The resurrection plant doesn't need to be rooted in soil because it takes all its nourishment from the air. During the rainy season it has lush green fronds. When the weather is dry, it turns brown, curls up in a ball, and looks dead. However, as soon as raindrops touch its leaves, the resurrection plant uncurls and turns bright green.

You can grow the resurrection plant as a houseplant. It's sold as a curled-up ball of dried leaves. Place the ball in a dish of water and watch as it magically transforms itself, within hours, into a soft, fluffy, green fern.

Let it dry out, and watch the plant turn brown, curl up, and go back to sleep. In this state it can survive for years without a drop of water. You can then transform it into a beautiful houseplant, just by placing it in water–no soil needed.

The Venus Flytrap

Charles Darwin, a scientist who made a lifelong study of plants and animals, called the Venus flytrap the most amazing plant he had ever seen. It grows wild in a small coastal swamp in North Carolina–and nowhere else in the world.

The Venus flytrap attracts insects with leaves that are shaped like a bear trap, baited with a special odor attractive to flies, and colored bright red as an added attraction.

When an insect lands on it, the trap springs shut in the blink of an eye and captures

A Garbage Garden

Many of the fresh fruits and vegetables that your family brings home from the supermarket have seeds that will grow into beautiful houseplants. Seeds found inside oranges, grapefruits, and lemons are very easy to sprout in moist potting soil on a kitchen window. They produce beautiful, dark green, glossy leaves and fragrant flowers. After several years, they may even produce fruit.

Venus flytrap

around your finger, which you can easily pull loose. You can even feed your Venus flytrap tiny pieces of hamburger if you don't think there are enough flies around to keep it happy.

the insect. The insect is then devoured by the plant's digestive juices. The Venus flytrap eats insects as an extra source of nitrogen, since the swampy soil where it grows in the wild rarely has enough nitrogen for the plant to survive.

The Venus flytrap makes an attractive houseplant. In spring it may even flower, sending up a long, flowering stem topped with white, daisy-like blossoms. The plant is harmless to people and pets. In fact, you'll have fun poking your finger in the traps, stimulating the trigger hairs, and watching the trap shut

Grow an Avocado Tree

The large, pointed seed inside an avocado will sprout even without soil. Just suspend the seed, pointed side up, in a jar of water by sticking toothpicks around the sides to support it over the jar.

The seed will split after a few weeks, sending out a root into the water and a shoot with green leaves that grows straight up.

toothpick

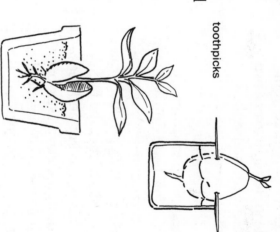

toothpicks

some leaves from the top of the plant. This will encourage your avocado to grow side branches. Otherwise, it may continue to grow a single long, slender stem that is not as attractive as a bushy plant. Keep cutting back the tips of side branches. In nature, avocados grow into very large trees, so pruning to keep your plant small and bushy is important.

Grow a Pineapple Plant

When you get a pineapple from the supermarket, you'll see that the top of the fruit is a spiky crown of pointed

When the shoot is about six inches tall and has developed more than one set of leaves, transplant it into a pot with potting soil. Cut

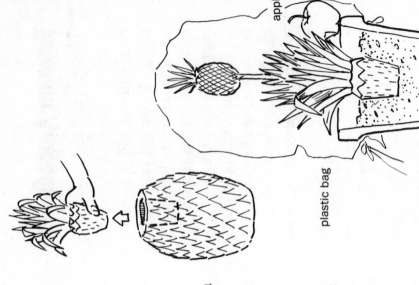

apple

plastic bag

leaves. Usually, you slice off the crown of leaves and throw it away before eating the pineapple But if you save it, you can help it grow into another pineapple plant.

Under the crown of leaves is a fibrous core All you need to start growing a new pineapple plant is to cut away the crown with a part of the core attached. Allow it to dry overnight. Then set the core in a pot with potting soil (a sandy potting soil is best), and put the pot in a sunny place The core will develop roots and the crown will develop new leaves. Always let the soil dry out before you

water it again. Feed your pineapple plant every two weeks with houseplant fertilizer.

It takes a long time for a pineapple plant to produce fruit. After two years, you can try to encourage your pineapple plant to produce fruit in the summer months by enclosing the pot and the plant in a clear plastic bag, with a ripe apple inside the bag. The apple gives off a natural gas that can encourage the pineapple to develop a fruit stalk from the center of the leaves. If it doesn't work after two years, try again the next year

Free Plants from Stem Cuttings

In Greek mythology, Hercules had to fight a monstrous sea serpent called the Hydra. The Hydra had nine heads, and every time Hercules chopped off a head, two more grew in its place.

Some plants are like the Hydra–if you cut them up, they will grow back as more plants. Coleus, purple heart, Swedish ivy, Tahitian bridal veil, and ti plants all grow well from cuttings. Just cut the stems into sections about four inches long and place them in a jar of water The cuttings will soon begin to develop vigorous new roots.

When the cuttings have developed good root systems, you can plant them in pots. Make sure to keep the soil moist, and soon you will have even more plants to decorate the house.

More Plants by Layering

Some houseplants produce side shoots that grow baby plants at the end. In some varieties, shoots grow next to the main plant. In other plants, they grow at the end of long stems. The best examples of these are the spider plant and the strawberry begonia.

The spider plant sends out dozens of long, flowering stems. The stems quickly form new plants at the end, complete with leaves and small roots. As these baby plants become heavy, they bend down and hang below the parent plant, creating a beautiful cascade

You can create more plants by layering them. Press the baby spider plants into pots with moist potting soil and allow them to take root. After about two weeks, you can snip the new plant away from its mother and it will grow into an adult spider plant and start sending out its own baby spider plants. Sometimes you can just snip away the new plant and pot it, but the baby plant is more likely to survive if it remains attached to its mother for at least two weeks.

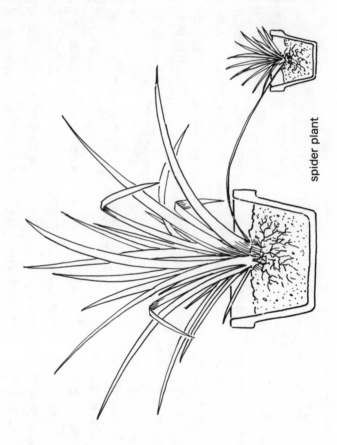

spider plant

Gardening
in
Small
Spaces

Even if you don't have room for a large garden, you can grow lots of flowers and vegetables in containers. If you choose plants such as vines that grow up instead of spreading sideways, you can train them to climb walls and fences.

Containers in many shapes and sizes are sold at garden centers. Inexpensive containers can often be found in junkyards or at auctions.

The bigger the container, the less watering the plant will need, and the easier the plants will be to grow. Small pots generally need watering daily to prevent them from drying out. Hanging baskets also dry out quickly and will need watering at least once a day. You can easily tell if a pot needs water by pinching some soil at the edge of the pot with your fingers. Moist soil will cling to your fingers. If it feels dry, water immediately.

It's important that pots for growing plants have holes in the bottom to let excess moisture drain away. If water is allowed to puddle in the bottom of a pot, the plant's roots will start to rot.

Plants grown in containers also need fertilizer more often than plants that grow in the ground. Usually, an application of fertilizer mixed with the water every two weeks will keep container-grown plants healthy.

Garden centers sell potting soils made especially for

container gardening. Potting soil works best if you mix it with an equal amount of garden topsoil before planting.

Here is a list of some good plants for growing in containers and small spaces:

FLOWERS
alyssum
begonias
coleus
geraniums
hyacinths
impatiens
marigolds
petunias
scarlet sage
verbena

VEGETABLES
beans (snap)
beets
carrots
cucumbers
  (dwarf)
lettuce
parsley
peppers
tomatoes
zucchini squash

Begonias, coleus, and impatiens grow well in shaded areas. The rest of these plants should be put in a sunny spot.

Windowsill Gardens

To garden on a windowsill it's best to use a container called a windowsill planter or a window box. You can usually find them at garden centers.

Windowsill planters are good for growing flowers, herbs, and salad greens. Lettuce, dwarf marigolds, nasturtiums, petunias, and impatiens are all easy to grow in windowsill planters.

Some windowsill planters have holes for drainage, but some do not. If a windowsill planter doesn't have drainage holes, fill the bottom of the container with small stones or broken pieces of clay pot. Then put a strip of cloth over them. This allows excess water to go through, but keeps soil from falling into the space

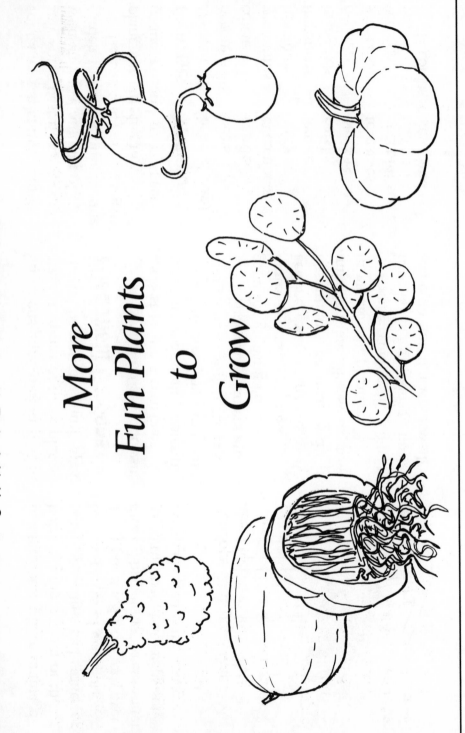

CHAPTER THIRTEEN

*More
Fun Plants
to
Grow*

H ere are some more ideas for plants to grow, and some fun gardening projects to try.

MAKE AN EGGHEAD WITH GREEN GROWING HAIR. Cut

the top off an eggshell and fill it with soil. Then paint a face on the shell. Plant lettuce, grass, or cress seeds on the surface. Keep the shell in a warm, dark place and water it regularly. Your egghead will

start to sprout green hair in about a week. Then you can put it on a windowsill to get some sun. When the hair gets long, you can give your egg-head a haircut with a pair of scissors.

INDOOR CRESS GARDEN.

Next time you get pies or packaged produce from the store, save the trays. You can line them with dampened paper towels and sprinkle curlycress seeds on top. By the next day, the seed coats will split, and within a few days the seeds will sprout healthy green leaves. A shady window is the best place for your cress garden.

After about ten days, the leaves will be large enough to cut and eat. You can use them as a tasty garnish to add flavor to soups, sandwiches, salads, and omelets.

MONEY PLANT. A beautiful,

purple-flowered plant called lunaria (loo-NAYR-ee-uh) develops seed pods that look like silver dollars. In fact, another name for lunaria is the silver dollar plant.

In autumn, the pods ripen, shed their outer skin, and reveal a shining, white disk. You can dry the disks and hang them as a decoration by the fireplace or in the kitchen. You could even try to sell

can grow them in your garden or on a sunny patio in six-inch pots. The plants produce yellow, pea-like flowers. As the flowers are fertilized, they magically form a long, slender probe that digs into the soil to form the peanuts underground.

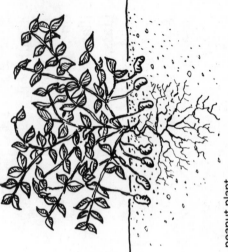

peanut plant

bunches of dried silver dollars to local stores and make *real* money. The plants re-seed themselves and usually come back year after year.

SENSITIVE PLANT. Mimosa, also called the sensitive plant, is so sensitive that when you touch it the leaves fold together in the blink of an eye. In the wild, mimosa grows in windy places, and it has developed a sensory system that closes up its leaves so that the wind does not damage them.

Mimosa grows easily from seeds, or you can find the plants ready-grown in pots at local houseplant outlets. In frost-free areas mimosa can be

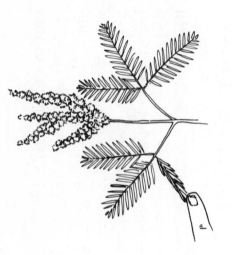

mimosa

grown outdoors, but in most places it should be grown as a houseplant, either in a sunny window or a lightly shaded place.

PROBING PEANUTS. Peanuts are not really nuts—they're related to peas and beans. You

When the plants die in the fall, just pull up the whole root and you'll see the peanuts attached to each underground shoot.

Unless you live in the South, where peanut seed can be purchased from garden centers, the best source is a mail-order vegetable catalog.

Usually, peanut seeds are packed in their shells. You can plant the seeds in their shells, but it's better to take them out. One shell can contain up to four seeds, so your packet will go further if you take them out of the shells first.

A good way to eat peanuts, besides roasting, is to boil them in their shells in water for 15 to 20 minutes and eat them as hot snacks after removing the shells.

BUILD A PUMPKIN FORT. It's fun to build a fort and plant pumpkin, gourd, or melon seeds around the sides. All you need are four posts covered along three sides with chicken wire. The vines will grow quickly and cover the fort, making it a good hideout and place to play. You'll also enjoy watching the vines flower and grow fruit–pumpkins for jack-o'lanterns, gourds for decorating, or melons for eating.

BEAN WIGWAM. Pole beans love to climb fences and poles.

bean wigwam

vegetable spaghetti

You can make them grow into a wigwam. All you need to do is set five or six tall, strong wooden poles in a circle and bind them together at the top with string. Then wrap string or wire around the poles, all the way up the sides. Plant Kentucky Wonder or Romano pole beans around the outside, and soon the vines will cover the wigwam. You'll enjoy playing in it and picking the beans and eating them.

VEGETABLE SPAGHETTI.

You can grow your own spaghetti on a vine that looks like a squash plant. (Vegetable spaghetti is also called "spaghetti squash.") The vine produces oval-shaped yellow fruits that look like melons.

When they are ripe, pick the fruits and bake them in the oven at about 370 degrees for 40 minutes. Then slice the fruit in half, scoop out the seeds from the center, and unravel the spaghetti with a fork.

You can pile it piping hot onto a plate, add spaghetti sauce, butter, or grated cheese, and you will hardly be able to tell the difference between vegetable spaghetti and regular spaghetti.

The fruits of vegetable spaghetti can be stored for a long time in a cool place.

CHOCOLATE PEPPERS. A plant scientist at the University of New Hampshire developed a pepper plant that produces fruit the color of chocolate. Of course, the peppers don't taste like chocolate, but they are so sweet you can eat them just like candy.

What's more, they're even easier to grow than regular green, red, or yellow peppers because chocolate peppers can take cool weather better than other peppers.

You can play tricks on your friends by offering them a bite of your chocolate peppers and see their surprise when they find out that they're not really made of chocolate

THE GOLDEN EGG TREE is not really a tree—it's an egg-plant, related to tomatoes and peppers. It produces fruit that looks so much like hen's eggs that you can't tell them apart without touching them.

The golden egg tree is easy

to grow from seed. You can grow the plants indoors or in the garden, as long as they get plenty of sun. To grow them outdoors, start the seeds indoors about six weeks before planting in the garden. The plants can be set into the garden after all danger of frost.

The golden egg tree grows quickly and produces lots of white, star-shaped flowers. The flowers then turn into the egg-shaped fruit. When you pick them, peel off the skin and cook the inside as you would a regular eggplant. They're especially tasty fried like fritters.

In some seed catalogs the

golden egg tree is listed as the Easter egg plant, in the eggplant section. Some mail-order catalogs also supply young plants.

golden egg tree

They make excellent bird-houses and table lamp bases when dried. The big gourds can be found in many shapes, from flying saucers to crooknecks and turbans.

Gourds are easy to grow. Plant the seeds one inch deep in a sunny place. The plants produce long, rambling vines that can take up a lot of space. You may want to plant them next to a trellis or a fence, so they can grow upward. The seeds germinate quickly, first producing decorative yellow flowers, followed by the beautiful gourds. Just 80 to 90 days are needed from seed to harvest.

FANCY GOURDS.
Gourd gardening is great fun because gourds grow in so many shapes and colors.

There are three kinds of gourds. The small fancy gourds are shaped like eggs, pears, oranges, or even small bottles. You can dry and varnish them for colorful indoor decorations. Bottle gourds are bottle-shaped, with a long neck.

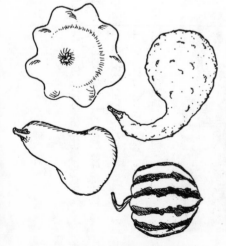

You can purchase seeds from mail-order catalogs. Since they are used for decoration and not for eating, they're usually listed in the flower seed section.

SKYSCRAPER SWEET CORN.
The stalks of this giant corn grow as high as 16 feet, so tall that you'll need a stepladder to harvest the corn. The cobs grow up to 28 inches long.

It's best to plant the corn directly into the garden. Plant the seeds one inch deep, leaving six inches of space between plants. Space the rows three feet apart.

Before producing ears of

corn the corn plant grows a flower on top of its stalk, called a "tassel," and some silky threads from a leaf joint about halfway up the plant, called a "silk." When pollen from the tassel falls onto the

skyscraper sweet corn

silk an ear of corn grows below the silk.

Sweet corn prefers lots of sun, a fertile soil, and plenty of water at the time the tassels and silks appear, so that the resulting ear of corn can grow plump and sweet.

You can tell that the ear is ready to harvest and eat when it feels plump and full of kernels, and the silk on the end has turned brown.

STRAWBERRY POPCORN.

Most popcorn is yellow or white. But plant breeders have now developed a popcorn that is strawberry-red. You can dry it to use as a Thanksgiving decoration, and you can also

pop it in the oven or micro-wave. You can even pop the corn right on the cob.

When it pops, an in-credible change occurs: the red outer skin folds under, and the snow-white interior fluffs out, so that instead of red popcorn you end up with popcorn that's pure white and very tender and delicious.

Glossary

Annuals (AHN-yoo-ulz) Flowers that sprout, flower, and produce seeds in the same year, but do not return the following year.

Bacteria (bak-TEER-ee-uh) Microscopic creatures that live in the soil and help to create plant food.

Bulb A swollen area of stem or root where a plant stores food in order to survive the winter. "Bulb" is also used to describe a plant that produces a bulb, such as a tulip.

Compost pile Kitchen wastes (such as potato peelings) and garden debris (such as grass clippings) that gardeners collect and let decay into a fluffy material rich in plant food. Compost can improve poor soil.

Deciduous (deh-SIJ-uh-wuss) Trees such as maple and elm that shed their leaves in the fall and then grow them back in the spring.

Evergreens Trees that keep their leaves all winter. There are needle evergreens, such as pines and spruce, and broadleaf evergreens, such as holly and rhododendrons.

Germination (jer-muh-NAY-shun) The process by which a seed sprouts. Seeds need moisture and air in order to germinate.

Herbs (URBS) Plants that are grown for their useful properties, such as a pleasant fragrance or flavor, or a healing benefit.

Humus (HEW-muss) A spongy material made up of decaying animal and plant matter. Humus is usually rich in plant food.

Hybrid A cross between two types of animals or plants. Plant breeders sometimes create bigger, stronger, or faster-growing plants by crossing different kinds of plants.

Loam The best soil for growing plants. Loam is soil that contains both coarse and fine particles and is rich in plant food.

Mulch A layer of straw, grass clippings, wood chips, or leaves spread over a garden to prevent weeds from growing.

Mutation (mew-TAY-shun) An accident of nature that produces a new type of fruit, flower, or vegetable.

Nectar A sweet liquid produced by flowers. Bees make honey from nectar.

Organic (or-GAN-ik) Made of plant and animal matter, without man-made chemicals.

Peat A light, fluffy material made of decayed moss that is dug from deposits deep in the earth. Gardeners like to mix peat with fertilizer and add it to garden soil.

Perennials (puh-REN-ee-uhlz) Flowers that keep coming back year after year from roots that rest in the soil through the winter.

Plant Food Nutrients in the soil that plants need to grow. Plant food is produced by creatures such as earthworms and bacteria that break down particles in the soil.

Pollen A fine, powderlike material produced by male flowers. In order for many fruits and vegetables to grow, pollen must be transferred from a male flower to a female flower.

Pollination (pol-ih-NAY-shun) The process of transferring pollen from a male flower to a female flower. Often, bees transfer pollen as they go from flower to flower drinking nectar.

Sapling A young tree.

Spade A large shovel, used for turning over the soil.

Tendril A curly stem that vines and climbing plants use to attach themselves to things.

Trowel A small shovel, used to plant seeds and young plants, and to dig up weeds.

Sources

Seed & Nursery Catalogs

The following seed and nursery companies publish mail-order catalogs offering many of the seeds and plants described in this book.

W. Atlee Burpee Company
200 Park Avenue
Warminster, PA 18974

Features mule marigolds, cut-and-come-again zinnias, hardy hybrid hibiscus, gloriosa daisies, African amaryllis, elephant's ear, daffodils, "Supersteak" tomatoes, Tri-Star strawberries, hybrid poplars, beans, money plant, vegetable spaghetti, pumpkins, peanuts, gourds, and cress.

Comstock Ferre & Company
263 Main Street
Wethersfield, CT 06109

An especially good source of seeds for herbs; also seeds for annuals, vegetables, and perennials.

Henry Field Seed & Nursery Company
407 Sycamore Street
Shenandoah, IA 51602

Good listings of seeds for annuals and vegetables; also trees, shrubs, and perennial plants.

Gardeners Choice
Box 25
Hartford, MI

Catalog includes mule marigolds, hardy hybrid hibiscus, elephant's ear, "Supersteak" tomatoes, cabbage, all-seasons strawberry, "Earliglow" strawberries, hummingbird vine, hybrid poplar, Australian hybrid willow, resurrection plant, golden egg tree, chocolate peppers, money plant, skyscraper sweet corn, and strawberry popcorn.

Gurney Seed & Nursery Company
Yankton, SD 57079

A colorful catalog full of unusual flowers and vegetables, including blue potatoes.

Joseph Harris Company
Moreton Farm
Rochester, NY 14624

An excellent source of flower and vegetable seeds.

Johnny's Selected Seeds
Box 100
Albion, ME 04910

Specializes in vegetables to grow from seed, including purple-podded beans and chocolate peppers.

Earl May Seed Company
Shenandoah, IA 51603

Catalog features seeds for annuals and vegetables; one of the few seed sources for "O.S. Cross" hybrid cabbage.

Mellingers, Inc.
North Lima, OH 44452

A good source of seeds for many unusual kinds of flowers and vegetables, including a tall, climbing tomato.

Spring Hill Nurseries
6523 North Galena Road
Peoria, IL 61656

Specialists in supplying flowering bulbs; also fruit trees, berries, and perennial plants.

Stokes Seeds, Inc.
Box 548
Buffalo, NY 14240

Superb source of vegetable and flower seeds; also offers seed-starting supplies such as Jiffy-7 peat pellets.

Thompson & Morgan
Box 1308
Jackson, NJ 08527

Very colorful catalog featuring seeds for rare and unusual plants, including annuals, perennials, vegetables, trees, and shrubs. Listed in the *Guinness Book of World Records* for offering the world's largest number of seed varieties.

Magazines

Flower & Garden, published bimonthly. $8.00 per year. Subscriptions Department, 4521 Pennsylvania Avenue, Kansas City, MO 04111.

Horticulture, published monthly. $26.00 per year. Subscription Department, Box 53879, Boulder, CO 80321.

Organic Gardening. $18.00 per year (10 issues). Subscription Department, 33 E. Minor Street, Emmaus, PA 18098.